THE AMERICAN CENTURY SERIES

DOWNTOWN
PROVIDENCE
IN THE TWENTIETH CENTURY

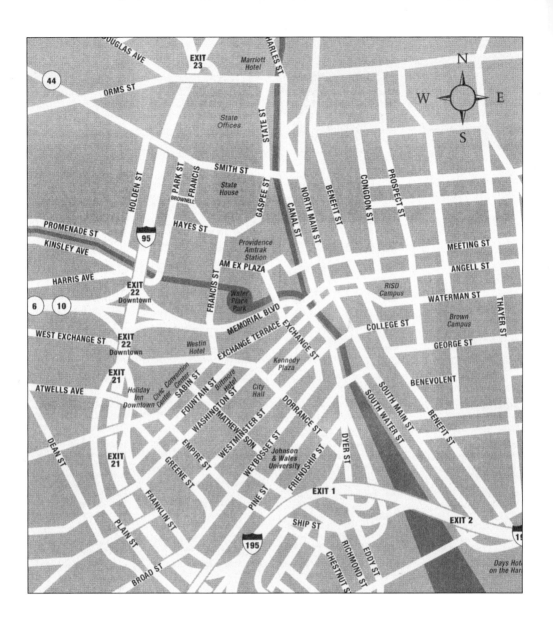

being restored; the empty, cavernous Masonic Temple—looking like a birthday cake on a hill—is being reoriented as a glassed-in shopping center with an atrium. A great river is being restored end to end, and more movies are being filmed here in 1 year than had been filmed in 20 years. The movie industry is finding that Downtown Providence is really Hollywood East, along with places like Newport, Warwick Neck, the East Side . . .

This is a city changing by the day. It is an enthusiastic, colorful, safer city, more than it has ever been. It is fresh and new, and people, typically reflecting that New England reluctance to go very far, many of whom have not been to Downtown Providence in years, are going Downcity, and are finding a city of extraordinary beauty, variety, and culture. Newly restored bronzes grace Kennedy Plaza, monuments to the wars of the past and the men who fought them; the stages of theaters have been widened, given greater depth to attract the big shows the spectaculars; and little theaters crowd against each other, each offering a unique, different living theater experience. Wherever one looks, one sees murals, wall decorations, trompe l'oeil dazzling illusions, museums, numerous galleries—this is the city of today. Everything is here.

And not to be forgotten is the Downcity of Yesterday with its great crowds, its teeming factories, its plentiful department stores, its rows of theaters, movies and vaudeville, the Bijou, Fay's, Carlton, Strand, Metropolitan, Albee, etc. It is a city where presidents and would-be presidents have come, Kennedy, Eisenhower, and Clinton, and where Truman stood in his open car with a smile as dazzling as the sun, where Adlai Stevenson wept at Union Station, and where movie stars such as Bacall, Bogie, and Ryan accompanied these memorable politicians. That was the past, the old past and the recent past, not to be forgotten. Women working in the factories during the war, celebrations marking the end of wars, parades, the rolling wave of immigrants pouring into the city and its environs, the richness of so many languages, the English and Irish, the Germans and Italians, the French and Portuguese, Greek and Jew, Armenian, and now the Hispanic, Russian, Asian, and African, a myriad people drawn to Downtown. It is a melting pot not as vast as that of New York. No pretensions are made. But it is a crucible where so many from so many places have met, worked, laughed, played, and enjoyed the day, are still doing so, and where a renaissance is now extending a noble welcome to the 21st century.

By Joe Fuoco

DOWNTOWN PROVIDENCE

Downtown Providence ("Downcity") has always been the mecca, the great attraction, the hub, the vortex. Itself a small commercial and arts area, already old and flourishing by 1900, it has been the place for gathering, shopping, eating, movie going, working, or just walking about, decades before Petula Clark made the whole idea of "Downtown" popular!

This book examines the Downtown area of Providence from roughly the year 1900, focusing on changes that have taken place through the 20th century and taking a look at this city now called the Renaissance City for its forward movement into the 21st century. Many of the old buildings are there, and a look from a planned perspective presents a dramatic panorama of architecture spanning over 100 years. Yet, Providence has always been an Italian Renaissance city, and the influence of Italian Renaissance architecture abounds in its facades, great cornices, Corinthian columns, and replicas of Italian palaces. The city is Italian in its look to the core, embellished by nods and curtsies to Federalist and Colonial styles.

Downtown has always been the place for theater and movies, for the First Run. The sprawling malls and multi-screens of the suburbs closed many of the theaters in the Downtown area. That is true. But memory, and the archives, prove a time when no less than 24 theaters flourished in the Downtown area. As this book is being prepared, a planned cinema of no less than 12 screens is breaking ground, and also two great projects are underway, the Providence Mall and a separate theater in the Arts District. Today, artists are drawn to the mecca because of the abundance of arts, and they occupy newly refurbished lofts in emulation of Soho, of the Village.

Here, once, Caruso sang, Toscanini conducted, Gigli warbled, and legends like Helen Hays, the Barrymores, etc., played out their comic/tragic roles on stages long demolished. A few relics, preserved and restored, echo that era: the great Loew's State, now the Providence Performing Arts Center; and the exquisitely tiled and stain-glass–domed Majestic, now Trinity Rep theater, renowned all over the world. Old churches remain, gothic splendors, and the river has been unearthed. The great Woonasquatucket has once again been joined at a confluence with the Providence River, and what existed in the 18th century has been restored. New bridges cross the river, there are walks and lanes, and Waterplace Park is celebrated across the country for its beauty and design. Finally, Downtown Providence has again earned the title "The Venice of the North." Again, as this book is being prepared, ground has been broken for a splendid outdoor ice-skating rink close to majestic City Hall. The rink will be three times larger than Rockefeller Center's. For a small city, people think big, and that is fitting. Old buildings are

The American Century Series

Downtown
PROVIDENCE
in the Twentieth Century

Joe Fuoco and A.J. Lothrop

ARCADIA

Published by Arcadia Publishing,
an imprint of Tempus Publishing, Inc.
2 Cumberland Street
Charleston, SC 29401

Printed in Great Britain.

Library of Congress Catalog Card Number:

For all general information contact Arcadia Publishing at:
Telephone 843-853-2070
Fax 843-853-0044
E-Mail arcadia@charleston.net

For customer service and orders:
Toll-Free 1-888-313-BOOK

Visit us on the internet at http://www.arcadiaimages.com

This volume of memories and images is dedicated to our mothers,
Florine Fuoco and Lynn Fisher.
Florine for decades worked in the old Newbury and
Woolworth Department Stores, now gone, and
Lynn worked in the coffee and sundry shop in the magnificent Fleet Center.
By all accounts, they both knew or met
"everybody in the city."

CONTENTS

ACKNOWLEDGMENTS

Again, it is necessary to thank several sources for their generosity and work, for this book would have been impossible otherwise. Thanks to the RI Historical Preservation Commission for invaluable historic photos, to Josephine De Rotto for her personal glimpses, and to A.J. Lothrop, co-author and photographer, whose work was, as usual, essential.

The magnificent State House, built of granite, looking like a miniature Washington Capitol. Recently cleaned and restored, it was used by director Stephen Spielberg for his film *Amistad*, largely filmed in Rhode Island. The RI State Capitol building is considered one of the most beautiful in the country.

A big celebration in the plaza, later called Kennedy Plaza. This was just after World War I ended. Many of the buildings and sculptures in this photo, dating from about 1916, are still standing. Notice the bunting high on the buildings.

Union Station, a superb set of buildings now used as offices and restaurants. During the Depression years, to put men to work, the building was covered with battleship gray paint! Now its beauty has returned and it is a key player in the Renaissance City.

Beneficent Church, commonly called Round Top Church, a Neoclassic edifice, one of the oldest in Downtown Providence. It too has undergone a splendid restoration.

The mayor of the town. Vincent (Buddy) A. Cianci Jr., the energetic, dedicated mayor, is famed for his vision and love of Providence. Behind him stand some of the city's skyscrapers.

The city at night, a beautiful, dramatic sight from Prospect Park, one of the high points in the city. Far in the distance is the Westin Hotel; closer is Citizen's Bank; and to the left are the Industrial Bank Tower, City Hall, and the Biltmore, spanning more than 100 years of architecture. The historic houses in the foreground creep up the beautiful streets of the Brown University area.

The Rhode Island School of Design (RISD), one of the most prestigious art schools in the world. RISD occupies some of the most beautiful historic buildings. This is one of them, situated at the bottom of College Hill. It looks as if it was built yesterday.

The historic John Brown House. Located on Brown University, it is not in Downtown proper, but to exclude it would be to ignore RI's most prestigious name, that of the Brown's. Educators, religious leaders, manufacturers, slave traders, etc., the Brown family is indispensable in Rhode Island history. This house, open to the public, has some of the original wallpaper on view.

The state capitol at night. Looking like a
misty wedding cake, its dome is the fourth
largest in the world. Atop it stands the
Independent Man, a symbol of Rhode
Island's historical go-it-alone philosophy.

Westminster Street in the busy
Downtown of the early 1930s.
Most of these buildings still stand.
To the right one might glimpse
the columns of the Arcade, the
first shopping "mall" in America,
its columns of solid granite,
monoliths carved whole.

A turn-of-the-century parade in Downtown. The crudeness of the float is offset by the beauty and patrician bearing of the riders. Notice the old E.L. Freeman sign.

When Johnny comes marching home. These soldiers returning from the Great War were photographed in the Downtown plaza. Perhaps none of them could ever conceive of another war, since this was called the War to end all Wars. Of course, it wasn't.

Historical Preservation Commission.)

The Exchange Bank Building in 1915. This imposing Victorian building is still standing. The curving arches on the left are part of the Turk's head building. The Turk is clearly seen in another photograph in this book.

The Lonsdale and Francis Buildings, built in 1894, Westminster Street. Notice the superb, graceful Ionic columns, single pieces of granite of the Arcade, its facade resembling a Greek temple. (Courtesy of the RI Historical Preservation Commission.)

The old Providence Journal Building in 1903. Looking like a too embellished French Chateau, the Journal was located for most of the 19th century on lower Westminster Street. In 1906, it moved to the corner of Westminster and Eddy. In 1934, it again moved to Fountain Street. (Courtesy of the RI Historical Preservation Commission.)

A building that was burned and then rebuilt. The photo, from 1890, was taken the year before the fire. These are the Dorrance and Gaspee Buildings on Westminster Street, a retail corner where ladies' spring coats, suits, wraps, and jackets were sold. (Courtesy of the RI Historical Preservation Commission.)

Is there a more famous store than Shepard's? Probably not, at least not in Downtown Providence. Elegant, as famed for its clock as its Renaissance arches and magnificent interior, it is still in use, but no longer as a top-of-the-line retail store. Founded in 1880, the Shepard Company once occupied the whole block bounded by Westminster, Clemence, Washington, and Union Streets. (Courtesy of RI Historical Preservation Commission.)

The Slade Building on Washington Street. Today, this is a very colorful, striking building, with its tower-like corner multi-colored, reminding one of a Florentine tower. (Courtesy of the RI Historical Preservation Commission.)

The Rhode Island Hospital Trust National Bank (1891), Westminster Street. A beautiful Renaissance-style building, it was unfortunately demolished in 1916. (Courtesy of RI Historical Preservation Commission.)

The famous Conrad building, its turreted curving stories still very much occupied as beautiful apartments. Located on the corner of Westminster and Aborn Streets, this remarkable and unique building was built in 1885, a piece of investment property that represented the growth of personal wealth. (Courtesy of RI Historical Preservation Commission.)

The George C. Arnold Building in 1923. This corner has seen a lot of action through the years. Next to it, the wall with the arch is the old Paramount Theater, now closed. Once showing the latest De Mille gaudy spectacle (or Gloria Swanson descending that staircase!), the Paramount became home to raucous rock groups, street fights, and general pandemonium. But fairer hopes abound. (Courtesy of the RI Historical Preservation Commission.)

The Banigan Building (built in 1896), Weybosset Street. At the time it was built, it was unique in that it was the most modern structure in Providence, ten stories of steel frame, a "fireproof" building. It was really Providence's first skyscraper. (Courtesy of RI Historical Preservation Commission.)

28

Union Station in 1848. Exchange Place sprawls before it. Behind it is the Cove Basin, alternately filled in, then recently unearthed as the core of the superb Waterplace Park. (Courtesy of the RI Historical Preservation Commission.)

The Industrial National Bank Building. Built in 1928, it is 26 stories high. It is unquestionably Downtown Providence's best-known landmark, and the only remaining skyscraper from the 1920s. Its Art Deco styling and detailing are masterful. This was built even before the Chrysler and Empire State buildings in NYC.

The Arcade (built in 1828). Six great Ionic columns (each one a single piece) crown the south side of the Arcade, the oldest shopping mall in America. The other side is a mirror image. The Arcade has three floors of shops, restaurants, galleries, etc. and was the first commercial building built on the Weybosset side.

The Greater Providence Bank Building, once called the Union Trust Company building (1901). With an opulent look, ornate, splendid, and masterful, of infinite variety, this twelve-story-high building was once the tallest building in the Downtown area.

A dramatic view of Downtown Providence from Prospect Park high above the city. What you are seeing is nearly 300 years of architecture represented. The park offers the most spectacular panorama of Downtown.

Tunnels beneath a building belonging to the RISD complex. These tunnels exit on College Hill, Thayer Street. Busses allow easy and quick access from the Downtown to the University area.

A striking picture from the late 1940s, looking toward the Federal Building and the historic church steeples in the distance. To the right is massive City Hall; to the left is the Biltmore Hotel.

Two

CLANG, CLANG, CLANG WENT THE TROLLEY

Trolleys that were used to scale the precipitous College Hill. This is Market Square in the years 1898–99. Notice the counterweights on the cars to assure their safety as they rose and descended. (Collection of Joe Fuoco.)

An 1895 scene in front of the Union Railroad waiting station in Market Square, Downtown. A variety of trolleys are seen here, including the Jones single truck box 60. Market Square was then the very center of business in Downtown Providence, and the trolleys congregated here, passing through.

Exchange Place. "Things moving" is the best way to describe this scene. The photograph was taken on September 8, 1908, during the celebration of "Old Home Week." The trolley in the foreground is a 1906 Cincinnati open 1463.

A mess on Weybosset, Richmond, and Mathewson Streets in the Downtown area. It seems as if every trolley ever built is here in this spectacular turn-of-the-century photograph.

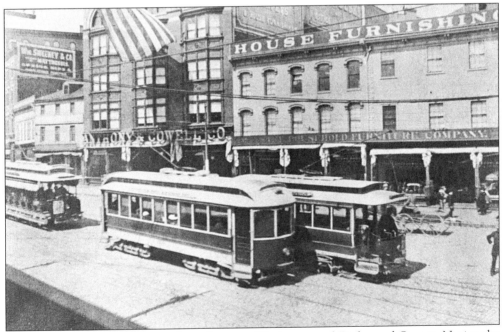

A c. 1900 scene of Downtown Providence at Weybosset and Richmond Streets. Notice the open and closed trolleys, and the horse-drawn carriage in the right background.

The squeaky clean interior of a trolley. People had no choice but to face each other in this style of trolley. The seats were rattan! These trolleys rolled along in the middle 1920s.

Two conductors standing proudly by an elegant trolley at the North Main Street Car House. These trolleys were built for the Providence & Burrilville Street Railway and were equipped with train doors.

A trolley, its antenna traveling an overhead wire, crossing Memorial Square in 1936, on its way to North Main Street. This trolley was called a Laconia 1635.

Another interior view, and a different kind of trolley. The seats were still rattan but offered some degree of privacy. At least, you didn't have to have eye contact if you didn't want to. Notice the curving rows of ads, and the pulleys to signal you wanted to get off.

The ever-present railroad station in 1936. The station serves as a backdrop for a trolley loading on Francis Street. Every car had a number, and this one, on its way to Chalkstone Avenue, is 1848.

A trolley enters the portal of the East Side Tunnel, traveling from Downtown. Above, one can see the historic buildings and houses of the University area.

An outbound trolley on Westminster Street at Empire. The war was over, and in 1946, the city was alive. At this time, both streetcars and trackless trolleys were running. Notice the wirework. In the distance is the Industrial Bank Building. Once there was a Bijou theater. The sign is to the right. The theater is gone.

The magnificent dome of the RI State House, looking like a roof ornament. The trolley is on its way on Francis Street in 1946.

A gathering place for trackless trolleys (resembling busses) and the older variety. This is the morning rush hour at Exchange Place, 1946.

One of the first freight cars built by the Union Railroad. It is on the Crawford Street Bridge (1901). It was later converted to a switchman's car.

Three

KILLER STORMS

A photograph of Dorrance and Weybosset Streets at 6 p.m. on September 21, 1938. The Great Storm (hurricanes were not named then) barreled up the East Coast from the tropical, boiling turbulence of the Caribbean and swept into New England. Downtown Providence was inundated.

The kind of currents that swept many to their deaths. If you look closely, you will notice a man struggling against a wall, center.

Marooned workers. From an arched window, blurred figures may be seen, people looking in disbelief at waters rising higher and higher.

A view of a parking lot at the corner of Eddy and Pine Streets. Yes, those are cars, the ocean and salt combining to make them forever inoperable. In this very lot, a girl drowned in her car.

The Eddy Street side of the Outlet Company. In those days, Providence had three major department stores, and all were inundated. The Outlet Company has since been demolished.

The Livermore and Knight Company (right) and the river, flowing up Pine Street. The company is gone.

Lethal timbers, not just floating twigs. They struck the first floor windows of buildings, acting like battering rams. This is lower Dorrance Street.

The Greek temple–like Arcade (far left), looking desperate as the waters of the Great Storm rise. It had reached 6 feet at this point. At its height, the Providence River rose 18 feet above the average low tide level in a record three hours! In all, the Great Storm took 317 lives.

The roofs of cars. The horror is that some people perished, stranded in cars submerged like these across Orange Street, dubbed the "canal" because of the water.

Gasoline pumps submerged in water at a gas station on the corner of Dorrance and Pine. This was not a good time to run out of gas.

City Hall, a refuge for the stranded. Notice the height of the water reaching halfway up a trolley. The storm struck with intense suddenness, and without warning.

Harris Furs, the place to go for furs of all kinds. Built in 1903, in what is known as the Caesar Misch Building, Harris remained at this spot for many, many years. The building, recently restored, is one of the most beautiful in the Downtown area. A legendary music store, Muffett's, was an occupant. (Courtesy of the RI Historic Preservation Commission.)

Tilden-Thurber. When one thinks of excellence and undisputed refinement, one thinks of Tilden-Thurber, to this day! Built in 1895, this was the store for fine jewelry and silverware, the hallmark of excellence. (Courtesy of the RI Historical Preservation Commission.)

The Burrill Building on Westminster Street. During the heyday of the growth of department stores, the beautiful Burrill Building was erected. This was the home of Gladding's, an upscale women's store that remained at this spot for decades. (Courtesy of the RI Historical Preservation Commission.)

The Outlet Company. Now demolished (on its spot is a beautiful campus, part of the Johnson and Wales University), this was the Santa Claus store. He might show up anywhere else, but the Outlet was his real venue! The Outlet competed with Shepard's until the latter closed in 1974. (Courtesy of the RI Historical Preservation Commission.)

A spectacular view of a World War I parade on the vast Exchange Place. To the left, unseen, is City Hall; Union Station is to the left rear. The photo was taken in 1919. (Courtesy of RI

City Hall, also bunting clad, with a flag composed of human beings, patriots all, for a "Preparedness Parade," June 1916. The Great War was still a few years from ending.

The elaborate bunting on the Equitable Building (built in 1872) on Weybosset Street, part of the celebration in 1886 of Providence's 250th birthday! This building, intact in what is considered by many the most beautiful section of Downtown Providence, is of cast-iron facade, one of the few remaining in the country. (Courtesy of the RI Historical Preservation Commission.)

The Hay Building and Owen block, built in 1867–68. This is the corner of Dyer Street. It is intact to this day. Notice the clear shot of the Industrial Bank Building in the distance with its "smoking" tower. (Courtesy of the RI Historical Preservation Commission.)

Exchange Place in 1883. Little remains today. City Hall, far in the distance, is still standing majestically, restored and occupied. But the old railroad station to the right is long gone. It was built in the Italian Lombard Romanesque style and consisted of seven buildings. This was the first Union Station, completed in 1848. (Courtesy of RI Historical Preservation Commission.)

Another view of the old Union Railroad depot, built in 1867. The area is called Market Square. The depot was demolished in 1897. (Courtesy of RI Historical Preservation Commission.)

The new Union Station, built in 1898. This is the original look of the buildings, later painted over a ghastly grey. Today, it is again fresh, and its ochre-colored brick facade gleams. A skating rink is being built in the area in front of the station. (Courtesy of RI Historical Preservation Commission.)

The Stephen
Waterman House
(c. 1820) on
Weybosset Street. This
is a rare house in that
architect Greene
designed a third floor.
By this year, the
Downtown area was
thriving, and a lot of
money was being made
by entrepreneurs.
(Courtesy of RI
Historical Preservation
Commission.)

An engraving of Westminster Street looking east from Aborn about 1870. The graceful spire of
Grace Church can still be seen today. This street was to change greatly in the period of growth
in the Downcity area. (Courtesy of the RI Historical Preservation Commission.)

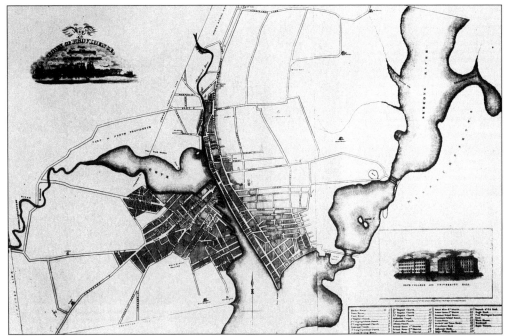

A map of Providence showing the expansion west through Downtown in the early 19th century. Notice the cove, which was to be shamefully filled in, only to be restored in recent years as part of the great renaissance of the city. (Courtesy of RI Historical Preservation Commission.)

The magnificent interior of the Industrial National Bank in 1928. Once the tallest structure in the Downtown area, its beacon is a smoking chimney. Notice the magnificent Ionic columns in the interior. This is the way it appeared on opening day in 1928. (Courtesy of RI Historical Preservation Commission.)

A beautiful, hazy, and nostalgic view of Downtown Providence from Waterplace Park. The uncrowded skyline makes the buildings unique, separate, and stark.

The Old Citizen's Bank in Downtown. Elegant, presumptuous, Victorian, and intact, it is one of the most splendid buildings in the city.

A parade. The St. Mary's Church Society of Broadway marches in Downtown Providence, passing the Butler Exchange building on Exchange Place, on its way to the reviewing stand of the St. Peter and Paul Cathedral.

The Benjamin Dyer block (*c.* 1820) on Weybosset Street. John Holden Greene was the architect. It is the only rowhouse he ever designed. This is a Civil War–era view. (Courtesy of RI Historical Preservation Commission.)

One

THE OLD CITY

A view of Downtown Providence—small, compact, fascinating, art-oriented, a Renaissance City. The Industrial Bank is the large building to the left. The Providence River flows in the foreground. The city has changed much since this photo was taken. (Courtesy of the RI Heritage Preservation Commission.)

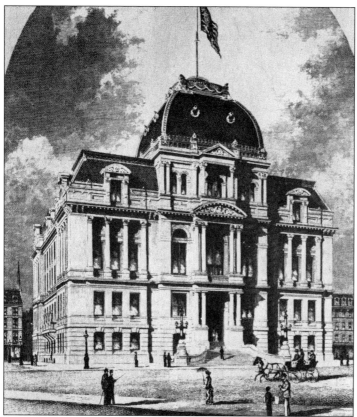

City Hall, facing Kennedy Plaza, built in 1874–75, located at 25 Dorrance Street. Designed by Damuel F.J. Thayer, this magnificent structure has changed very little in over 120 years. But it has been restored and cleaned, and its interior is a masterpiece. (Courtesy of the RI Heritage Preservation Commission.)

City Hall today, proving that virtually nothing has changed since its creation. Splendid, stately, and majestic, it is one of the more pristine edifices in the Downtown area.

High as it might be, the Biltmore Hotel's first floor with its high ceilings still "went under," for the water rose here to 7 feet.

Everything at a standstill. Abandoned trucks and trolleys in Exchange Place demonstrate just how suddenly the storm approached. Even Union Station lost its roof (right).

The Central Fire Station and the post office (both in the background). Luckily, nobody needed any fires put out, and it was definitely not a day to mail letters.

The great Civil War Monument, an inveterate survivor. The monument seems to float on the waters in the Mall, later renamed Kennedy Plaza. At this very spot, a man drowned.

Two views of the same spot. Here is a store at Dorrance and Pine at the height of the water. Ironically, a boat was rowed out of the window of this boat supplies store in an attempt at rescue.

And the morning after at the same corner. Looking dry as a bone, people still seem stunned, and even alien in a city that has become equally strange and foreign.

What many car and truck owners found when the waters went down. Parking was only 15¢ an hour, and 25¢ all day, but what was there to park?

A toppled truck near the Union Trust Building. Imagine the force of water needed to accomplish this. Even the street lamp is bent as if in deference to the storm.

A Downtown parking lot. Topsy-turvy, smashed, nearly impaled by beams, cars that are now historic were cast about indifferently.

After the storm. The receding water left debris, garbage, barrels, beams, etc. in a tangled mass.

The area near the Point Street Bridge. No, this is not a river near a lumber camp, but the area near the Point Street Bridge, where millions of feet of lumber were swept from waterfront yards and thrown against scows that were not going anywhere.

Three Full Pages of Pictures Pages 6, 7 and 8

Fair and Mild Today,
Clear and Cool Tonight

Today's Tides:
High 11:08 p.m., 10:22 p.m.
Forecast for Rhode Island by Boston
U.S. Weather Bureau at 11 a.m.

The Providence Journal

HURRICANE EXTRA

VOLUME CXXVI. NO. 209.   TWENTY PAGES   PROVIDENCE, RHODE ISLAND, WEDNESDAY, SEPTEMBER 1, 1954   PRICE FIVE CENTS   25 Cents Per Week Delivered by Carrier

Hurricane Leaves 16 Dead, Scores Hurt, $100,000,000 Damage Along R. I. Coast

Rhode Island Casualties

DEAD

BELAND, John W., 34, of 456 Pequot Drive, Oakland Beach, drowned.
GALLO, Culberine, about 72, of 7 Pallas St., Providence, drowned in Oakland Beach area.
GALLO, Francesco P., of 7 Pallas St., Providence, drowned in Oakland Beach area.
HERTEL, Mrs. Pauline J, of Seven Oaks, Hope Street, Bristol, drowned.
JACKSON, Matthew B., 63, of Garper Point Drive, Warwick, sudden.
MARSLAND, Richard, 47, of 333 Broadway, Pawtucket, sudden.
HEFNER, Miss Maud, of Hurricane Hut, Ocean Drive, Newport, a cook for Mr. and Mrs. William Van Alen.
HERVEY, William, 45, of 28 Farm St., Cranston, died last night at St. Joseph's Hospital from broken bones and internal injuries suffered when blown off a roof in Cranston.
McGOLDRICK, Frank, same address, a chauffeur for the Van Alen family.
O'BRIEN, Trooper Daniel L., Rhode Island State Police, drowned.
PETERSON—A man, no other identification, drowned.
UNIDENTIFIED — Two persons reported drowned at Island Park. No identification.
A third employe of the Van Alen, unidentified.
UNIDENTIFIED WOMAN, about 60, found at Galilee near the trash fish plant, wearing a green life preserver.

Devastating Blow, High Tides Mash Houses, Piers, Boats

By STUART O. HALE

Rhode Island lies wounded this morning in the wake of a devastating hurricane which ripped its coastal communities into shreds, mashed houses, docks and boats to splinters and left a mounting toll of dead and injured.

Early today at least 16 persons were known dead and scores were injured.

Initial estimates placed property damage at more than the $100,000,000 hurricane of Sept. 21, 1938, until yesterday the greatest storm to strike the state in modern times.

Most of the state was without power throughout the night and spokesmen for the Narragansett Electric Company, the principal power source, expected little improvement today.

The front page of the *Providence Journal* on September 1, 1954. Now hurricanes had names, and this one, Carol, an echo of the Great Storm of '38, did its own damage, killing, maiming, destroying. This one came and went so fast, it was like a dream. It still took 19 lives. There have been other notable storms, such as the Blizzard of '78, and a host of hurricanes, but the Great Storm of '38 is the true legend of storms. (From the book *Hurricane Carol*.)

Four
The Enduring Renaissance

A great arch that might be found in any Italian city. This arch is in Downtown Providence, gracing a corner of the former Shepard Department store. Coffered, with a rotunda-like interior, it is one of the beauties of the Italian Renaissance restoration of Downcity.

A cornice to rival any of the Old World. If one does not take the time to look up in Downtown, one misses an architectural heritage unequalled on the East Coast.

An elegant, small marble column. This probably doesn't hold up much of the Met Cafe, still a very popular watering place, but its decorative capital is unique.

The stunning entrance of a former bank, now a restaurant. Ornate, lively, almost musical, arches, decorative figures, and Corinthian columns are outstanding examples of the Italian Renaissance Downcity.

Another great arch with a sunburst design. No, those are not real owls who have found a nesting area or at least a predatory advantage in an elegant setting. They are sculptures to scare off indiscriminate birds.

Ionic columns, symphonies of marble, elegant levels that are a delight to walk. Few buildings are as impressive as City Hall, restored to a glory that has to be seen.

A sweeping staircase in City Hall. From any angle, including this powerful photo, the great architecture of the Renaissance is celebrated.

Balance, proportion, drama, a sweeping cascade of stairs, all hallmarks of the Italian Renaissance, proudly celebrated in City Hall. The impact is stunning.

Stair angles, cornices, the bowed glass roof, marble columns, and decorative, symmetrically designed railings—all speak majestically of the Renaissance. The architectural core of City Hall is created about an atrium.

61

The Providence Central Branch of the Public Library. Strangely, this magnificent, powerful entrance had been closed to the public for years, in less enlightened times, during what might be called the "plastic age." But wisdom and an appreciation for architecture and art has returned bountifully, and the doors of this beautiful facade are again the way in.

Another view of the Providence Public Library, main branch. Notice the brilliant light illuminating the west side of the facade. This is one of the most beautiful buildings in the Downtown area.

A mural on the wall of the former Strand Theater. Murals are popping up all over the city, and this one, on the wall of the former Strand Theater, may be lost to the construction of a multi-screened theater complex. Nevertheless, it is an example of the return to wall paintings that reflect an art form going back to ancient Rome and Pompeii.

The elegant symmetry of the Arcade, with more contemporary buildings behind.

Undergoing its own renaissance. Not all of the buildings look pristine, but fairer hopes. This one, as of now, is undergoing a splendid renaissance of its own. The top story is a later addition, but its overhanging cornice is definitively Renaissance.

Another view. This side is in better condition and illustrates what potential there is in this beautiful facade.

The restored Shepard Department Store, now owned by the University of Rhode Island. This corner, a dramatic shot appearing at the beginning of this chapter, is one of two gracing the corners of this superb building. In its day, Shepard's was considered the most beautiful of the department stores Downcity.

An example of what can be done with a flat wall. The Italians knew how to take a flat wall and do something with it! Never boring, always intense, and dramatic with a quality bespeaking empire, this building might be standing in Florence.

A Florentine temple transplanted, in a manner of speaking. This small, elegant, striking building next to the Arcade is modeled after an Italian mini-palace. Its beauty is seamless.

A study in Renaissance restraint. Strictly modeled after designs by Michelangelo for his Florentine palaces, so that the third story is slightly different from the others (a true Michelangelo innovation), this building of red brick is a treasure.

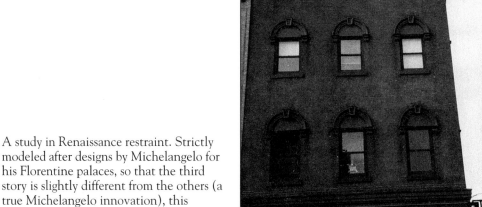

A simple, uninspired building. As sedate and as unobtrusive as its unhurried and unimbellished decorativeness, there is still a quiet glow against the facade of this simple, inspired building.

A corner that is easily a lesson in Italian Renaissance architecture. The restoration of the indispensible beauty of Downcity architecture goes on.

A false wall. Like a page ripped from a sketchbook, this wall, but for the top penthouse, is phony, a bow to fool the eye brilliance of the High Renaissance and Baroque periods.

Another wonderful entrance. The wonderful Neoclassic entrance of this ornate building and its columns evoke the architecture of the Renaissance. Forget the mailbox in the corner.

Five

OF STAGE AND SCREEN

Trinity Rep. All that is necessary is to say Trinity Rep, and people know! Nearing 40, this is the premier acting company of Rhode Island. Daring, often controversial, courageous, and brilliant, it is celebrated throughout the world and is housed in the magnificent former Majestic Theater. This photo, from a production of *Angels in America, Part II: Perestroika*, shows some of the resident talent. From left to right are Brian McEleney, Anne Scurria, Ed Shea, Jennifer Mudge Tucker, and Ray Ford. (Courtesy of Trinity Repertory.)

Downtown in 1947. Over a half century ago, Downtown Providence was *the* place to go for films, opera, plays, and fantastic dining. It is all coming back. This page illustrates perfectly what was "playing," and who was doing the playing, everybody from Laurel and Hardy to Bing Crosby, via the elegant and patrician Gene Tierney. (Collection of Joe Fuoco.)

Cats at PPAC (Providence Performing Arts Center), once the revered Loew's State motion picture theater. This massive Baroque theater seats over 3,000, and with an expanded stage, it now brings into Downtown spectaculars like *Cats, Miss Saigon, Les Miz,* and of course, *Phantom of the Opera.* To think this magnificent theater was once slated for demolition is now absurd. It is an indispensible anchor on Weybosset Street. (Courtesy of PPAC.)

Serious drama. It must be Russian . . . maybe. At Trinity Rep, this is Bob Colonna on the left, son of the famed moustache-adorned Jerry Colonna, and actor/director Ed Shea. (Courtesy of Trinity Repertory.)

The Providence Opera House on Dorrance at Pine Street. Built in 1871, this great theater, now demolished, heard all of the great voices of the day, the great orchestras, and the legendary conductors. It remained Downtown's leading legitimate theater well into the 1920s. Even earlier, Howard Hall, also on Dorrance, presented people like Jenny Lind, Edgar Allan Poe, Tom Thumb, and Sam Houston. The only thing that eclipsed stage performances was the advent and subsequent popularity of the motion picture in the 1920s. (Courtesy of the RI Historical Preservation Commission.)

Myles Marsden Ballet Company 5th Season

Myles Marsden. An arts city without dance is unthinkable. Years ago, impresario/dancer Myles Marsden graced the stages of Downtown Providence with his ballet company, the State Ballet of RI. Famed and well received, it was, for Providence, innovative. Myles, long away, has returned, and he and his wife, Linda, now toil as managers/agents, operating an acting school and representing screenwriters. This is Myles, who still dances, striking an intense, dramatic pose.

The Strand Theater in 1919, built in 1916. Originally a silent movie palace, it is fitting that in the 1950s Gloria Swanson was seen here on screen descending that famous staircase in *Sunset Boulevard*. De Mille's awful epics also splattered the screen in their day. The Strand eventually closed and suffered an ignominious period of rock shows, street riots, etc. (Courtesy of the RI Historical Preservation Commission.)

The Strand today. The architecture of the building is intact, fortunately. But the Strand, as of this writing, is closed, a casualty to contemporary diversions! Still, there are plans to salvage the old theater. Next to it, on an empty lot, a a six-screen cinema is planned.

The Majestic Today, with a "new" name, Trinity Repertory. The famed acting company, winner of international awards, has done well by the old Majestic, and vice versa. The beautiful tiles are still there, glowing in the morning sunlight. The theater is alive!

The Majestic Theater, known for its superb tiles and its magnificent second-floor rotunda with its stained-glass dome. The movies are gone, but Trinity Repertory is well established in this beautifully restored building on Washington Street. Over 50 years ago, Tyrone Power and Gene Tierney professed love in the *Razor's Edge*, while Anne Baxter suffered mightily on a silver screen in this theater. Today, one might hear and see things impossible a half century ago. C'est la vie!

Nearly lost to the wrecker's ball. Did Judy Garland and the notoriously talented Margaret O'Brien really sing and dance on screen here? You bet. And in 1940, Scarlett and Rhett tore through a burning Atlanta. Before the awful name Ocean State Theater was ever put on a sign, this was Loew's State Theater, the most elaborate and palatial in Downtown Providence.

But saved! The shrine to the silver screen, opened in 1928, has become the magnificently preserved and restored Providence Performing Arts Center. In a city developing several blocks of an arts district, theaters such as Trinity Rep and PPAC are essential, along with numerous smaller theaters, no less professional.

Josephine De Rotto. On the stage of the nearly lost Veteran's Memorial Auditorium, Josephine De Rotto, the well-known soprano, sings her heart out in the 1960s. The theater, known throughout the country for its impeccable acoustics, was the theater for opera and concerts. Maestro Danilo Sciotti led many an orchestra and singer through their paces in Verdi warhorses in this theater, now restored to its former beauty. Maria Spacagna, the Met Opera star and native Rhode Islander, has sung here. (Courtesy of Josephine De Rotto.)

Salty Brine. What is a Salty Brine? In this case, the question is "Who is Salty Brine?" Only one of the best known and beloved of entertainers and television personalities. Here, in a relatively new career, he comforts the heroine of *Guys and Dolls*. Salty really held court in the old Channel 10 TV studios in Downtown Providence for decades. (Courtesy of Theater by the Sea.)

Different gown, same venue. Josie, as she is known, is singing, by her own account, either a Verdi or Puccini aria. Along with PPAC and Trinity Rep's superb theaters, Veteran's Memorial maintains its unparalleled acoustics and is home to the RI Philharmonic. (Courtesy of Josephine De Rotto.)

One of the many choral groups. The RI Civic Chorale, the Brown University Chorus, etc. all have graced the Downtown theaters. The old Albee, demolished, was home to choruses for decades. Here, a chorus of singers, all employees of Brown and Sharpe, give a concert in the late 1940s. (Courtesy of Josephine De Rotto.)

Delores Mitchell (left) and Trinity's Barbara Meek portraying the Delany sisters in a production of Emily Mann's *Having Our Say*. Of this splendid acting company, a resident of Downtown Providence, no less a legend than Katherine Hepburn, remarked, "It is a jewel." (Courtesy of Trinity Repertory.)

A final look at a page torn from the annals of the heyday of motion pictures. The sheer number of Downtown theaters is mind boggling, but over 50 years ago considered quite ordinary. Virtually all of these theaters are gone. In fact, not one motion picture theater is left Downtown. Hence, a multi-screen complex is in the works. (Collection of Joe Fuoco.)

Six

CHANGES IN THE CITY

The old Rhode Island College of Education (once called the Normal School) and adjoining structures being razed. A proposed spectacular mall called the Providence Place Mall is now well under construction on the site. This is *the* major change Downtown.

The Hurricane Dam, which, since Hurricane Carol, has at least spared the Downtown area the tragic flooding of the Great Storm of '38.

The great foyer of the Fleet Center. The marble interior is striking and superbly balanced. Concerts are often given in this elegant space.

The construction of Citizen's Bank and Plaza close to Waterplace Park. Here the twin rivers, the Woonasquatucket and the Moshassuck, have been joined in a mighty undertaking, restoring the great basin and the confluence of the beautiful rivers that had been largely concealed for decades.

Another view of the building of the canal, now complete. The construction of new bridges, overlooks, parks, and elegant surroundings now makes the area a definite showplace.

Holding back the water as construction goes on. Notice the arch of one of the completed bridges. This completed project has created one of the most magnificent city areas in the Northeast.

The newest of the new hotels, the soaring, majestic Westin, turreted, a unique work of architecture close to the Convention Center and the Civic Center.

Another great undertaking, the clearing of a bus depot to create a skating rink. City Hall is to the right background. The rink will be 2.5 times the size of the rink at Rockefeller Center. They think big here.

A dramatic view of several buildings spanning more than 70 years of construction. Kennedy Plaza is at the foot of these buildings. City Hall is just out of view to the right.

A view of the business district, the Hospital Trust Bank, the Citizen's Bank, and other buildings near the small park on the left where Roger Williams is honored. The historic Moshassuck River is to the right.

The great monument to those who died in the Civil War. This powerful work, recently restored, may have lost its patina (as have other sculptures in the parks) but it has gained in beauty and durability.

A shot of the vast area where the new mall is being built. In the background, the Westin Hotel is visible.

The Federal Court building at the end of Kennedy Plaza. There are closeups of one of the great sculptures in another chapter.

The birthday cake-looking capital (right), the empty Masonic Temple (above it, now under restoration), and the rivers, which at the time were still separated. Before the great undertaking of Waterplace Park and the building of Citizen's Bank and Plaza, a major part of Downtown Providence looked like this. This scene was to change dramatically by the late 1990s.

The Biltmore Hotel, one of the city's landmarks. Historic and elegant, it has an outside elevator that offers a spectacular view of the city and the hills of Brown University. The hotel was opened in 1922, the very year King Tut's Tomb was discovered. Thousands of people attended the opening.

Cleaning and restoring. City Hall looks over Kennedy Plaza, with the railroad station to the left. In the lift, among others is former governor and senator John O. Pastore in the soft hat, and former mayor Joseph A. Paolino. The entire area is under renovation.

Westminster Mall, when it *was* a mall. Shoppers walk down what was once a one-way street during the conversion of this street to an inner-city mall. It didn't work.

Another view of the plaza under construction. The brick sidewalks remain, and so do many of the stores (though others have long closed), but the plaza today has been returned to a one-way street.

The construction of the sprawling Providence Place Mall. In the distance may be seen an Armenian church, the frame of the Masonic Temple, and the Veteran's Memorial Auditorium.

A college and a school of continuing education, down for the count. On this spot will rise the Providence Place Mall and a movie complex. The city is building upon the debris of the old and useless.

City Center Place, *the* place to live if you have the money in the Downtown area. With penthouses and magnificent views all around, the new railroad is to its right, the Westin Hotel to the left, and Waterplace Park at its feet. The design of this building may leave something to be desired, but its presence is formidable.

Seven
THE WORKPLACE

A very old photograph of a stately factory building. The Providence Steam and Gas Pipe Co. was ensconced here, but so were jewelry companies such as the W. Haskell Co, producing Rhode Island's most ubiquitous export.

The Providence Engineering Works on South Main Street at the turn of the century. Notice in the background an old gasometer from the gas company's Pine Street plant.

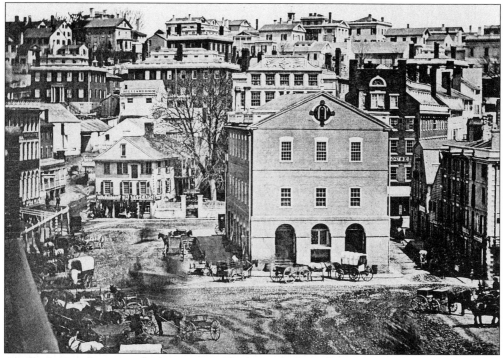

An illustration depicting the busy area at the base of what is known as College Hill. Many of the original buildings, especially the houses and mansions, are intact, creating one of the most beautiful sections of the city where the sprawling campus of Brown University is situated, along with the Rhode Island School of Design. This is one of the most historically preserved of areas. The small building to the left bears a sign saying, "Hats and Caps."

The Dabol Rubber Company. Most of the big factories touched the edge of what is now considered Downcity. Point Street was the area of many factories of varying sizes. The Dabol Rubber Company was one of the largest. Many additions since 1880 enlarged the company. Today, there is no rubber company, and there is no Dabol. Once developed as a storied indoor shopping mall, beautiful and innovative, with trendy bars and lounges and catwalks, it failed. (Courtesy of the RI Heritage Preservation Commission.)

A precision workroom at Brown and Sharpe. Unquestionably, the most famous of all the factories was Brown and Sharpe. This shot, from 1940, shows workers busy at the kind of precision tool manufacturing that made Brown and Sharpe famous.

The all-consuming Brown and Sharpe, a manufacturing company on Promenade Street founded by David Brown and Lucien Sharpe. The Woonasquatucket River flows by. This is the way the complex looked in 1910. Innovation was a hallmark of this company, which made precision tools. Precision gears were invented here, as well as a linear dividing machine. The

company grew from a small work force of 14 in the 1850s to 200 by 1868. In the 20th century, Henry D. Sharpe, son of Lucien, was a force in the company's growth. He stayed for 50 years. (Courtesy of the RI Heritage Preservation Commission.)

The Irons and Russell Building, 1903. Located on Chestnut Street, in the very heart of a crowded manufacturing district (jewelry was *the* product), this large jewelry manufacturing plant was built on the site of the Home for Aged Men. (Courtesy of the RI Heritage Preservation Commission.)

The New England Butt Co. (don't laugh; this was long before the word "butt" developed a more personal connotation!). One of the area's oldest manufacturing firms, founded in 1842, the New England Butt Co. cast iron butt-hinges, until they became obsolete. It then manufactured braiding machinery. (Courtesy of the RI Heritage Preservation Commission.)

A 1915 photograph of a room in a jewelry plant. This room looks neat, and everybody seems industrious in a clone-like way. The work was monotonous, body-numbing, and eye-straining, but jewelry was the biggest business in Rhode Island. Notice the floor man standing to the rear, left. (Courtesy of the RI Historical Preservation Commission.)

Laboring over files . . . and files, long before the days of the computer at the Brown and Sharpe Manufacturing Company. The men were off to the war . . . as usual. (Courtesy of Josephine De Rotto.)

And certainly all was not work. Known for its very fair treatment of its workers and a preferred place to work for thousands, Brown and Sharpe had its own chorale in the fifties. Here more than 40 entertain away from the factory. (Courtesy of Josephine De Rotto.)

The Providence Machine Company. This beautiful and detailed engraving is from 1886. Some unusual features of this factory are the four octagonal corner towers (only one remains) and a two-tiered cupola, since removed. (Courtesy of the RI Heritage Preservation Commission.)

An example of a kind of interior factory construction, pre-1920s. This photo shows the mushroom columns and flat slab construction that was replaced later on by reinforced concrete during the 1920s. This is the A.T. Wall Building. (Courtesy of the RI Heritage Preservation Commission.)

A beautifully lit photo from 1897. This is the interior of the Narragansett Electric Lighting Co. office at 60 Weybosset Street. The woodwork glows. (Courtesy of the RI Heritage Preservation Commission.)

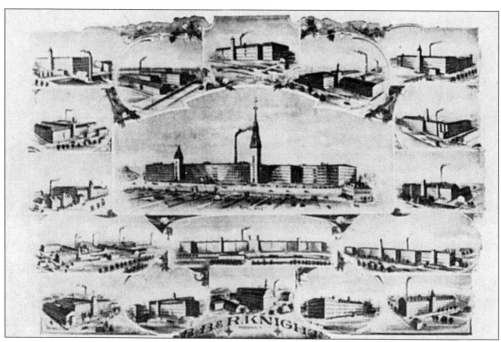

The holdings of Benjamin and Robert Knight. Mills bought up because of the bankrupt Sprague empire made Benjamin and Robert Knight wealthy. This illustration from 1910 shows the extent of their holdings. The offices were located on 3 Washington Row, Providence, but the mills were everywhere. (Courtesy of the RI Heritage Preservation Commission.)

Eight
WATERPLACE PARK
AND THE BRIDGES

Waterplace Park, the basin, and some of the walkways. A restaurant and tourist information center can be seen in the center, top. Close to the basin is a platform and a flood of stone stairs creating a theater area in the open-air Greek style. Bridges span the rivers that now meet to form the Providence River.

A view of the Woonasquatucket on its way to meeting the Moshassuck. The entire area of Waterplace Park, embankments, the courses of the rivers, etc. is a re-creation from the long ago past, before the basin was filled in and topped with, of all things, a parking lot! But the Renaissance city of Providence could not tolerate that insult.

The prow of an elegant, black-and-red-and-gold gondola. For a couple of years gondolas, steered by colorfully dressed gondoliers, have been carrying passengers, even newlyweds, along the river. A Water Fire display is also created every summer, a spectacular and moving experience.

A closer view of the centerpiece of Waterplace Park, with its cascading granite stairs, a clocktower, restaurant, and walks.

In winter, quiet, still water, reflecting graceful lampposts in the basin. In the distance cranes mark where the Providence Place Mall is being built.

A closeup of one of the superb bridges. Each contains plaques, decorative ovals, maps, and emblems, the names of all the cities and towns in RI.

A dramatic view from a lookout, peering under one of the graceful bridges, and arched walkways, looking toward the east side, historic buildings, and the big Citizen's Bank and Plaza.

Bridges spanning the Providence River. Notice the rows of torches. These are lit on summer nights as part of the illumination, along with the Water Fire displays. This entire area has now become the most beautiful part of Downtown Providence.

"Historic Benefit Street." Just up the hill to the right of the bridge is the Brown University Campus and buildings. It, and Benefit Street, are perfectly preserved.

George Street, the bridge spanning the Providence River, connecting Downtown Providence to South Main Street, and the east side. The whole of the project, Waterplace Park, the bridges, etc., has been an award winner, re-defining the area once known as the "Venice of the North." The title has been reclaimed.

The unmistakable, unofficial logo of a sailboat on the roof of a restaurant in Waterplace Park. Top center is the Masonic Temple, now under renovation, for decades a shell of a building, empty and unused.

One of the superb bridges spanning the Providence River leading to the complex of the Court House. At night, the bridges are lit, and in the summer Water Fire, a display that attracts thousands, makes the river shimmer.

An example of one of the many bridge pedestals, decorated with bronze plaques and the names of the streets crossing the bridges.

Nine

INTO THE
TWENTY-FIRST CENTURY

A dramatic view of the modern city, composed of old and new buildings. This view is close to
Waterplace Park, taken from the Citizen's Bank Plaza.

A stunning photo of the reflection of the Hospital Trust Building in the windows of another, making it look Central American, or at least Native American in design. The modern building looks as if it is growing out of the Old Citizens Bank. What a study in contrast.

A view from the plaza. Notice how the middle building with its step-like facade and large oval window looks as if its windows are highly decorated. They are not. This is a reflection of the building next door.

Talk about facades. No, this is not a peeling historic building, but all paint, a trompe l'oiel tour de force. What's real here are the tiny windows and the top floor, a penthouse.

Hospital Trust. Downtown abounds in variety of architecture, and sometimes the buildings, looking bunched, create a fascinating esthetic. Simple, stoic, high and beautiful in its symmetry, this is the Hospital Trust.

111

The police and fire stations. This is an old, antiquated, outdated building, soon to be torn down for a new, beautifully designed complex .

A great shot down an alley (many of Downtown Providence's streets are narrow, quaint). At the far end one can see the Florentine palace profiled in the chapter on the Downtown Renaissance.

Downtown's own gyrating cop, retired Tony Lepore. Once a year at Christmas, Tony takes his position as traffic cop on this oval of cobblestones. He whistles, pleads, cajoles, and does a Nureyev with panache.

Tony Lepore. Kneeling in prayer, or convinced of some vision, Tony stops traffic with a plea and a warning . . . and a whistle. He is one of the great attractions of Downtown Providence.

The monument to the soldiers of the First World War. The column now stands in a beautiful park where other war memorials are being built. Behind it are the buildings of the courts and other government offices. This monument faces the Providence River and the new bridges.

An example of mighty congestion. This area, often called one of the most beautiful Downtown with its superb buildings and the Arcade and Florentine temple to the left, sports a Christmas star. For a small city, the traffic and activity is impressive.

The Railroad Station, a replacement for the old station, now occupied by corporate giants, beer-making establishments, offices, etc. This building, sleek, with a beauty of its own, still does not make one forget its old murky, cold, dusty, but full-of-character predecessor.

The Old Stone Bank, no longer a bank. The building boasts a ceiling to rival some of the temples of Rome. Its golden dome is a landmark, and the beautiful building is now home to the Haffenreffer American Indian Museum.

A former toilet? Smack in the middle of Westminster Street in front of the old Loew's State (now the Providence Performing Arts Center), this ornate Victorian building has been renovated, cleaned up, and is now a police-maintained station.

One of the beautiful fountains in Burnside Park, Baroque, of stone and metal. The park is frequented by strollers, and for years it has even been a summer "home" for bag ladies and assorted homeless people. But that is changing.

Colonel Ambrose E. Burnside, resplendent in bronze. Burnside, the Rhode Island Civil War legend (he was commander of the Second Brigade, Second Division, Army of the Potomac as a colonel, and was later a general, governor, and U.S. senator), holds his binoculars in his hand as he looks over the terrain—Kennedy Plaza and a park named for himself. His last name and the wearing of burnsides gave a new word to the American language, sideburns.

Looking from the high and wide portal of City Hall on a day when young basketball players are honored. Events like these are common in this spot just before Kennedy Plaza.

The powerful facade of the Cathedral of St. Peter and Paul, seat of the bishop and the focus of a beautiful square. It is the largest church in the Downtown Providence area and is famed for its great rose windows, its stained glass, and its stunning coffered ceiling.

The *Providence Journal Bulletin*—the biggest paper in the state, Pulitzer winner, and the core of much argument (it is beloved and despised). It has been published daily since 1829, and its influence in Downtown politics, and in every aspect of daily life, is incalculable. Names like Brown, Watkins, Chafee, Metcalf, and Goddard (Blue Blood Yankees all!) denote the five fabulously rich families who were the absolute dynastic rulers until the controversial death of Michael Metcalf.

Bishop Louis A. Gelineau, for more than a quarter century the Roman Catholic bishop of RI. Now retired, he still maintains an apartment in Cathedral Square, close to the great church he served.

Downtown's hole-in-the-wall places. Many of these are located in historic buildings, on small streets, lending a special character to the area. This is Peck Place, named for the street it faces. It contains a superbly sculptured oval bar and has many sculptures, reliefs, etc. protected under glass. Its ambience is friendly, almost Old World, a charming place.

A real, down-to-earth, no-frills little bar on Dorrance Street. Notice the delightful molding.

Capriccio. The famous, renowned, and the infamous have all dined here. It is celebrated nationwide. Anybody who comes to Downtown Providence for the first time searches out this exquisite restaurant, located in a historic building not far from the bridges of the Providence River.

A former small factory. The interior wood and brick walls remain, beams intact, but the venue is very different. City Side Cafe is one of many sporting an old/new look.

City View, one of the grand upscale residences in the Downtown area. Overlooking Waterplace Park, with a splendid view of the buildings, this apartment complex is trés expensive, and very beautiful.

A look down Westminster Street. This photograph offers a view of an area known for department stores, apartment buildings, and upscale shops. The spire belongs to one of the most beautiful and historic edifices, Grace Episcopal Church, renowned for its organ. Next to it once stood the Albee Theater.

There are those who cared . . . deeply. Downtown Providence has its own walk of stars in front of the PPAC. Inscribed in the bronze stars are the names of those whose contributions to the saving of the magnificent Loew's State movie palace preserved a gem that now brings blockbuster shows to the city.

And here she is . . . one of a pair of matching symbols of justice, give or take a symbol or two. These sculptures have recently been painstakingly restored and are now in magnificent shape, guarding the Federal Building at the far end of Kennedy Plaza.

Downtown Providence's "empire state building." It certainly commands, in this view, a pose as dramatic and as irresistible as that of the Big Apple's centerpiece.

A beautiful view close to sunset of Downtown Providence far in the distance, from the vantage point of a lookout along the Woonasquatucket River.

A shot of the Hospital Trust with its Neoclassic first floor, and one of the bridges spanning the Providence River. This redesigned area of bridges is considered the most beautiful in Downtown, connecting with Waterplace Park at one end, and the Bay at the other.

Huddled, almost encroaching in this photo, some of Downtown Providence's buildings appearing cohesive, intimate.

A view from Prospect Park, looking toward the state capitol. The folly of the Masonic Temple is to the left, a folly already being corrected by beautiful, esthetic plans for conversion of this empty building to shops, restaurants, etc.

Finally, a most spectacular view of Downtown Providence from Prospect Park. There is no better view of the whole of the Downtown area. It is proof that the Renaissance City is alive and flourishing.